Fegan Method of Learning

6 Simple Steps that
Make Learning Fun!

Other Works by Rebecca Fegan

Spotlight on the Art of Grace

Spotlight on the Art of Resilience

Spotlight on the Art of Significance

Spotlight on the Art of Fear

Spotlight on the Art of Generating Energy (editor)

Spotlight on the Art of Gratitude

Spotlight on the Art of Speaking

Training workshops for Toastmasters District 24, 47, and 99

Copyright © 2022 by Rebecca Fegan

Edited by Mark Fegan and Therese Guy

First Edition

ISBN **978-1-387-43011-6**

Testimonials

"Excellent teacher. She teaches in a way that you can learn and understand. I would highly recommend her."

~Kathy M.

"Rebecca is an excellent teacher! She is very good at breaking down complicated concepts and is very patient with you during the learning process. A+!"

~Rhett L.

"Rebecca is a great teacher. She zeros in on your individual talents and needs. I must say, I'm doing better than I ever thought I would, and I know it is because of Rebecca's insights into her students and her knowledge."

~Betty S.

"I love having Rebecca as a teacher. She works at my pace and is easy to learn from. I have really enjoyed my sessions and would recommend her to anyone who wants to improve."

~Diana B.

Fegan Method of Learning
A Process of 6 Simple Steps that Makes Learning Fun!

Contents

Preface

<u>Who should read this book?</u>

Have your children ever been unfairly labeled? How soon do you want them to gain the tools they need to be successful? How long do you want them to continue to feel inadequate or stupid? It doesn't matter if they're first grade or twelfth. It's never too early, and it's never too late!

What have you tried? Online courses? Self-help books? Tutors? Do you hate parent-teacher conferences because they all start with, "Your boy/girl is such a good kid, but…"?

If you answered "yes" to any of those questions, then you've come to the right place.

If, however, you believe it's the teacher's fault, that your child is lazy or not very bright, or that punishment and deprivation are the only cure for bad grades, look someplace else.

My Promise to you:

I understand. I've been where you are. You know the value of a good education. You hate to see your child's options getting lopped off like dead branches on a sick tree.

You're worried that nothing can help and afraid that you are not qualified to work with your child because you haven't had the education courses.

But if you believe that reading this short book might be the key to getting your child up to and exceeding expectations,

I promise you this:

The process you will learn in this book can be applied to any field of study—academic, physical, and even emotional!

By the time you finish this book, you and your child will have at your fingertips a tried and proven process that gives assurance that anything learned will stick as long as needed!

Is it Simple? Yes! Is it Easy? No. Nothing worthwhile is. Don't Trust me, Test this process for yourself. I know it works! And once you master it, nothing will be out of your grasp!

Dedication

First of all, I'd like to dedicate this book to my parents, teachers who had an impact on three generations of teachers who influenced musicians all over the continent. They were the impetus of this system that I have used for half a century.

Next, I am extremely grateful for Anna Simpson and the Empowered Women's Inner Circle for their support, their advice, and their expertise.

I would also like to thank Christian Simpson with his Entrepreneurial Mastery Inner Circle and the Conscious Coaching Academy for their insight and the business acumen and the wisdom.

I especially appreciate Therese Guy and my amazing husband, Mark, for editing for content, for feedback and for a reminder why I'm writing this book.

And Finally, Thanks to the Alternative Book Club without whom I would never have tried to write a book!

Who am I and why do I have the answers you seek?

I am a teacher. I have been teaching for over 50 years…half a century! When I was growing up, my parents were music teachers and often gave lessons at home. I assumed that everyone in school was teaching the same way. Surprisingly, they were not.

I assumed the students learned the same way I learned. I didn't know until I was in college that I was also wrong on that assumption. While other students crammed for tests, I just reviewed my notes once. While others were pigeon-holed into categories, I cringed at the labels…Business Majors should never be musicians. Music majors should never take advanced literature classes or calculus. I couldn't understand why people thought I was cheating on my homework in classes outside my major field of study, and why they thought I couldn't possibly get A's on tests without advanced knowledge of the answers.

When I got out into the real world, (I actually began teaching as a freshman in high school, but now I was getting paid much more!) my students did so much better than their peers. But…They weren't looking at the <u>results</u> of the students' efforts. They were looking for someone that conformed to the "normal" practices of education. (I never used "normal" practices!) It was then I discovered why.

I taught my students to learn in the same way I will teach you. I believe the first thing you teach a new student is how to learn the material. You give them a process they can use in every situation and the assurance that it works with every subject the student wants to learn. The educators in college, however, don't teach teachers how to learn.

I want to share this process with the world. So yes, at some points in the book, I will give you the opportunity to get in touch with me to get a more detailed view of this process and how it can work with the special circumstances you or your child faces.

I'm not writing this book to brag. I want to help you solve a problem, change a perspective, and open a door to new experiences and a love of learning. I want you to understand this process so you can share this with your child. If this is helpful for you, I hope you will recommend this book and the other products and services I offer to people you care about. And if you want to dive deeper, we can look at either being part of a Think Tank or scheduling one-on-one coaching sessions. But the purpose of this book is to solve your problem and give you the tools you need to rise to the challenge.

You can reach me on my contact page:
http://www.feganmethod.com/

Chapter 1

What is the biggest challenge in learning?

 In a school environment, especially in the younger grades, there is a wide range of knowledge and experience among the children. How do you teach them? The most common approach teachers take is just to assume that all the minds of the children coming to school are empty—blank slates, as it were. What other assumptions can they make? They do not have sufficient information on the children's home life, their activities, or their intellect. If they assume that the children <u>have</u> been to a museum or an art gallery, been out of the city, or heard other languages, and they rely on those beliefs, then children who live under adverse circumstances get left behind. If they assume the opposite, no one gets left behind, but those with more favorable life circumstances are held back and cannot progress as quickly as they'd like. Which is better? Neither?

1

You, as parents, already know what your children have and have not experienced. You are familiar with the kind of language their peers and neighbors speak. You understand what games they play. Your children have been learning from the time they were born. Their minds are definitely not empty slates!

The biggest challenge in learning, then, is the perception that children know nothing and cannot figure out anything on their own. *Ridiculous*! Have you ever asked your 6th grader to fix your phone, your freshman to explain Twitter, or your toddler how to program the television? If so, then you *know* this perception is incorrect!

The other fallacy is that children are not resourceful or creative. Give them some colored pencils or crayons and a sketchbook or ask them to tell you a story. The older they get, the less they are inclined to do anything creative. Why is this? I believe that these skills are discouraged because of the presumption by the educational system that since children are blank slates, they must be told everything. Like I said before, this is not the case. The current system, however, is based on these beliefs. Children are not given the opportunity to express themselves creatively, be resourceful, or participate actively in their learning. This approach is to all the students' detriment. A wise man once said,

"If YOU tell them, they doubt, if THEY tell you, it's true." If all the information the students gain is because someone else told them, how are they engaging their thinking and learning skills? So, in the first twelve years of school, the teachers mostly work with *content,* and they don't teach children how to learn. This is where parents need to step in. In my 50 years of teaching, the first lesson I teach is how to learn the material.

What skill is most needed in learning?

The skills most valued are the ones pushed by pundits and gurus in education: memorization, prioritization, and execution. Which one of those techniques allows a person to learn the most and retain for longer than an eyeblink? Let's examine those.

If you go to self-help websites or the section in the library or bookstore, you will see that a great many gurus will focus on **memorization**. There is a person who invites one hundred people up on the stage and he asks them their names then later has them come up again in a different order and he gets all their names correct. What a lovely parlor trick! Two weeks from now, if someone were to ask this man if he knew any accountants (because he did attach their occupations to their names), and assuming he had at least two more demonstrations, out of three hundred people, he should be able to list about twenty-five. What if they asked how many of those twenty-five were women?

3

If you are learning facts, figures, and terms to pass a test, memorization is a good skill to have. How will that serve you a month after the test? How about a year? A decade? If you are learning facts, figures, and terms to understand a new field of study, you will be using those terms and concepts every day. Memorization might be the first step, but once you begin *practicing* with that information, it becomes inseparable from your memory.

Is memorization the best way to learn? No. It's only an initial tool that makes understanding the material easier. Information-dumping into the brain fades quickly if there is no use for it other than passing a test.

Next is **prioritization**. What needs to be done first? How well does that first step have to be mastered before moving on to the next? This is where the bottleneck occurs. Many students are stuck on the first thing that has to be mastered because they cannot comprehend how the first step relates to the success of a whole process. Vocabulary words and spelling words in elementary school can easily be learned for the test and lost in the dusty file cabinets of the mind because the student doesn't know when, for instance, the vocabulary word, acuity, might be the perfect word he needs to explain his thought process. In another example, because of the frequency of use, a student must understand the differences between the words: there, their, and they're. The words need to be used correctly in context so that the student can confidently post on Facebook, even if a grammarian is reading the post!

But many times, students get stuck on early steps and cannot proceed to the next level of learning, and therefore, they do not understand the point of the lesson. It would be like prioritizing the physics involved in riding a bicycle. If the child must learn about angular momentum, inertia, and friction before venturing out on the bike, it will never get ridden.

Prioritization has a place in learning, but it shouldn't be the first place. It tends to focus on the initial requirement and then the ripple effect takes other requisite skills and knowledge out of the process leaving many areas unexamined.

How about **execution**? The problem you face in execution is measurement. To what degree do you have to master the material? It largely depends on its complexity.

A basic understanding of arithmetic will allow you to balance your checkbook, but it will not be enough to figure out your investment strategy. Being able to stand on one foot is essential for some yoga poses but being able to do consecutive fouettes en pointe in ballet requires a great many more-involved skills. Four-year-olds can play soccer, but none of them can freestyle like a pro. So, in the assessment of executing skills, what is considered passing? If your child came home with a math test where he scored 75%, does he have a grasp of the material? Most teachers would pass him, but would that serve him later in school when the new material he'd learn would be based on how well he understood the material he only got a 75% on?

Execution might be a good measure of understanding, but it is difficult to determine to what degree. After a certain point, the student needs to improve <u>performance</u> rather than <u>competence</u>. So, these skills are helpful, but not as essential as most educators think. What is the most important skill then?

The most important skill is learning how to learn.
And that has never been taught to students or teachers ... until now.

THE BOTTOM LINE: YOUR CHILD IS NOT STUPID!

He/she just hasn't learned how to learn, and that's not their fault.

Chapter 2

Now what? Since we have determined that none of the traditional approaches to learning are effective, how do we make sure our children *learn* something in school? How can they get caught up? How can the doors of opportunity reopen?

Contrary to popular educational belief, every single class that your child will attend will relate to every other class he currently takes, the ones from previous years, and the information and experiences he has outside of school. And not only that, each and every class will be related to every other in the future as well.

Only in this current conveyor-belt method is all the information separated and unrelated. Only in this automated process that we have become accustomed to, do we think the things inside and outside of school have no relevance to each other. My husband tells me that some of his former students are amazed that they're actually <u>using</u> Algebra after graduation! This is NOT how learning is supposed to work!

It is <u>not</u> the individual skills, tenacity, perseverance, and constant review; it is <u>not</u> goals and objectives which only determine the endpoint; it is a *process* that determines the path the student takes toward those goals. It is a series of steps that integrates all the skills and knowledge your child already has that allows your child to understand and apply to a new set of skills and knowledge.

What do I mean by that? Imagine your child is playing baseball. The skills and knowledge needed to play the game have nothing to do with the uniforms, the cleats, the official measurements of the field, or the height of the mound. It does have to do with the awareness of the way the pitcher throws the ball, the speed and possibly the path of the ball, the feel of the bat, the weight and balance of the bat, the stance, the placement of the outfielders, etc.

What skills would you need to develop to do that as a little kid? You wouldn't find those in school, would you? I would disagree. The child is already thinking on a creative level, analyzing the opposition, evaluating the circumstances (how fast can I swing this bat to hit the ball?), comparing the opposing team to his, and figuring out how to hit the ball to that little kid chasing butterflies in center field.

When do children stop thinking like this and become automatons just regurgitating what they think the teacher wants to hear? It's when these thinking skills are discouraged and left unused because the educational system we have adopted is so far outside of reality. Can we change the way our children learn? Absolutely!

Then there comes the "BUT" thinking.

But what if my child is limited in his ability? The first question beneath that question is: Limited how? If I wanted to be a basketball star, go up against Michael Jordan or Larry Bird, 5'2 and 67 years old just isn't going to cut it. On the other hand, neither of them can sing as high as I can (being male and untrained.) Physical limitations can change the direction of your dreams and goals.

The second question beneath that question, and the more insidious of the two, is this: Limited *by whom?* If you look at statistical models of intelligence and ability, you will discover that there are way too many variables to be considered in a model with any predictive value. Let me use myself as an example.

Lump all the ladies between ages 60 and 70 together. Now what percentage of them are under 5'5" tall? Now how many of them are musicians? Now how many of those 60–70-year-old female musicians under 5'5" tall have music degrees AND business degrees? Now how many have been truck stop cooks? Now how many have taught ballet? Now how many have 5 children? Now how many live in the Midwest? You see? All those factors are essential to predict my success in any area of interest. They do the same type of statistical analysis of children. In the old Dr. Spock book, there was a table that broke down "normal" behavior for babies.

- ☐ 2 months baby coos
- ☐ 4 months baby smiles and interacts with parents
- ☐ 5 months baby rolls from front to back and back to front
- ☐ 6 months baby sits
- ☐ 7 months baby crawls

And so on and so forth. If you were to do an exhaustive study of babies worldwide, you might find 1 baby that does all those things exactly on the date stated in the book. I had one like that and she was even born on her due date! Then she got into Girl Scouts and accelerated her progress and was no longer the "normal" girl.

The graph for the "normal child" looks like this:

_____/_____

Every other child's behavior falls outside the norm. So, if your child is not "normal" that's average. That sentence doesn't even make sense. The graph has no predictive value at all. Labels assigned to people rarely describe the individual. The CDC has said that between 9 and 12% of children are designated as ADHD. We used to call that daydreaming and boredom. There are therapies and drugs and special programs to help them. But there are some people who label kids ADHD because it's a convenience. These people have no psychological training, and no formal diagnosis is made. They just tell the parents that Johnny can't sit still, and Lisa still sings in class.

The same is true for Autism. Most teachers do not know how autistic children think and label them as a special kind of learning disabled. There is no way teachers could learn enough psychology to understand every single child in their classroom, and no way they want to fill out special paperwork to teach children on their level instead of what some statistician says is normal. What happens to the children? They are limited by what other people think their capabilities are, not by what they can actually do.

I have a friend that loves to play ukulele. She can strum, she can pick, or she can sing, but she can only do one of those things at a time. She's been encouraged by many people saying, "Of Course, you can do that," and then they stand and wait for her to do it correctly. She's come to resent these people. Yet, I have seen her instruct a class through a set of movements while talking. It's the same skill, but she cannot relate that skill to the ukulele. She says, "I can't do counting." She counts all the time...IN KOREAN! One day, she will get brave enough to seek lessons and I will help her learn that skill.

The limit she has set on herself is that she cannot count, or she cannot sing and strum at the same time. She made that rule, and every time she tries, her mind, understanding this rule, will send mixed messages to her and she'll mess up. Then the brain cheers, "Yay! I made her mess up just like she wanted! The rule is: I cannot strum and sing at the same time, and we fulfilled her wish! High Five Little Grey Cells!"

So you see, many times the only limitations we have are imposed on us by others or by statistics. We believe these limitations and make them into rules.

When you are learning something new, you have to ask yourself:

1. Are there any physical limitations I have that would prevent me from learning this skill or information?
2. Are there beliefs I have adopted that make me THINK I am prevented from learning this skill or information.

If this skill or knowledge sought is desired with a passion, the level of performance can be set by the student, not the teacher, not the critics, not the naysayers. This is deep learning.

If we can show them how to use a process to keep what they need in their heads long enough to pass a test, and then USE it for the rest of their lives, isn't that better than regurgitating what someone else believes is important? If the student learns what is most important to him to move him toward his goals, does it really matter what the teacher thinks is important?

Would you teach a kid in a wheelchair how to do Taekwondo? What would you do with a colorblind child who wanted to be an artist? I have a blind friend who had his friend teach him how to drive. It was a harrowing experience, but there was no blood. Sometimes the only limitations a person has are those he imposes on himself.

If we can show them how, with this process, everything we learn can be used in multiple ways to enhance understanding, isn't that better than putting every subject in its own steel box?

If we can show them a process that helps them improve their skills and knowledge in a logical way that doesn't depend solely on memorization, execution, and prioritization, won't that give them a sense of accomplishment and confidence in their inner resourcefulness rather than make them anxious about going to school and getting labeled as somehow inferior?

Then, LET'S GET STARTED!

Chapter 3

Are you intrigued yet? We will be learning a process to solve a problem: how to accumulate knowledge and experience that gives us the tools we need to succeed in life.

You ask, "How can you guarantee this process works?"

Let me introduce you to a few of my students! For obvious reasons, I won't use their actual names.

Aaron's Story:

Aaron was a great kid! He was funny and had a great work ethic. He had IEPs (an Individualized Education Program) in nearly every class. They classified him as having severe learning disabilities.

He had just graduated from sixth grade and his band director informed Aaron's mother, Charlotte, that he should probably drop out of Band because he wouldn't be able to keep up with the other players. This made his mother mad. Charlotte came to me and was ranting about the nerve of that band director. I agreed with her. She was surprised. I volunteered to teach the boy.

Because this process doesn't depend on standards set by the educational community, his educational program was the same as every other student I had…start where they are and take them where they want to be.

I discovered that while he might have had difficulties in reading words, he had no difficulty in reading music. He could also figure out musical patterns by ear. In fact, one time he forgot his books and so rather than cancel the lesson, we examined scales. Once he understood the pattern, he figured out all twelve major scales. Most students have to spend a lot of time memorizing key signatures (the flats and sharps of each scale) and finger combinations. Aaron just played.

Over the summer, we worked on the marching music he had to play for the junior high band and how to march and play at the same time. Because he couldn't read words or take notes well in school, he'd developed his listening skills to a high level. Had we not considered this a skill to be used in multiple subjects, he would surely have gotten frustrated in music and quit. Because we did, though, he was able to learn large swaths of his marching music with relative ease by ear.

We continued his lessons throughout his seventh and eighth-grade years. At the audition for the high school band, we discovered that the elementary school band director had not told the high school band director of his assessment. As a result, Aaron passed his audition with flying colors. How big a deal was this? He was the ONLY freshman in the varsity band.

We had identified how he learned best. We applied the steps in the process that allowed him to learn at a much faster pace. We didn't compare what his diagnosed condition implied was possible and what he was able to do in reality.

This process works!

Gerald's story:

I met Gerald's mom, Kathy, through a teaching service. She contacted me and pleaded with me to teach Gerald. No other teacher believed that he had the mental capacity to learn guitar. He was labeled "high-functioning autistic." (This was a while ago and the psychological community no longer uses that label.) However, at that time, it was a diagnosis that brought up pictures of Dustin Hoffman in Rain Man. It was considered a specialized form of learning disability.

Gerald had been told all his life by everyone important to him (except his mother) that his brain didn't work right and all kinds of exceptions had to be made to accommodate him. He was avoided by his peers and teachers alike.

When Gerald got anxious, he would twist his legs, rock back and forth in his chair, and moan. He was afraid of making mistakes. Every time he got lost or forgot a fingering or a note (he was learning guitar) he'd say, "It's my stupid brain! It doesn't work right!"

17

Finally, I stopped him, looked right into his eyes, and said, "Your brain is FINE! It just doesn't work like theirs! We will work with the brain you have because you have hidden your super thinking power beneath that stupid excuse that others have given you." His mom was crying. He hugged me.

I made no changes in the process, I made no exceptions to his performance requirements. He could recite the process perfectly even after a year of my teaching him. We constantly looked at how the process could work in other subjects. We were always including non-musical examples of learning in his music lessons. We learned some Italian and German phrases; we learned some history related to the songs he played; we learned to divide in our heads to aid in counting. We'd make up lyrics to the songs to learn musical interpretation.

In his third year of study, he had already surpassed many students who had started guitar at the same time as he had. One day in school, the teacher was passing out math tests to the students and mistakenly gave him one. He took it. She realized her mistake and tried to take it back saying, "Oh Gerald, I'm sorry! I forgot about your brain problem!" Gerald had seen some of the questions on the test and realized he could do the problems. He looked her directly in the eye (which was out of the ordinary for him!) and said, "My brain is fine, thank you very much! It just doesn't work like yours." He took the test and was finished before half of the class and got a pretty decent grade.

Kathy told me that the school psychologist asked her if her son was faking his autism. She almost clobbered him!

It works!

If you see your child in these descriptions, you're well on your way to solving the problems, you just don't know it yet. You can book a consultation with me regarding classes available for you to start so you can get your child caught up or maybe even surpass the others in his or her class.

Contact me at https://www.feganmethod.com/consultation/

What constitutes learning?

What is learning, really? Learning is acquiring a tool that allows you to do a task. You learn arithmetic so that you have the tool to balance your checkbook or figure out the price per ounce at the grocery store. You learn English grammar and spelling so that you have a tool to write and speak clearly. You combine tools to make a process. You learn a new process that gives you the tool to start your car, back it out of the driveway, and get to where you want to go with a minimum of traffic tickets. The older you get the number and complexity of the processes grow. But, and here is the most important question, how do you learn?

Some processes, like those required in advanced math at MIT, take pages and pages of other internal processes. Some, like cooking an omelet, are short and require a physical skill with acuity to recognize certain stages of the process and when to continue. That sounds rather complicated, doesn't it! (Are the eggs mixed well enough? Is the cooking surface the right temperature? What kind of cooking surface do you have--does it require some type of fat to keep the eggs from sticking? What kind of cheese is it--quick melting or slow melting? Is the omelet ready to turn? Are the inside ingredients hot?) So though there aren't many steps in this process, it takes practice and experience to recognize what the next step is and when it should occur.

The process simplifies the steps needed to identify what the student knows and what he doesn't. It clarifies the way to make new material relevant, understandable, and integrated into the knowledge the student already has. And it makes it easier to use information taken from other subjects to learn new material.

Chapter 4

<u>Learning Process</u>

You probably already know what steps you need to take to learn something. Do you use the same steps every time you learn? I would bet you do not. How many steps do you think it takes? Oh…you read the cover of my book. In any case, here they are:

These are the actual steps I teach my students:

1. Identify what you already know
2. Try it
3. Identify what you don't know (because you tried it and there are some things you messed up.) Analyze what needs to be corrected.

4. Work on only those skills or information.

5. Gradually add the new stuff to what you already know

6. Congratulate yourself, now you know it!

In my education courses in college, I had one educator that insisted that it took *thirty-three steps* for a person to learn information and retain it for the longest time. I was flabbergasted.

I remember my first piano recital. (by the way, that isn't me in the picture.) I remember what I wore and how my mom fixed my hair. I remember that I had to sit on a couple of encyclopedia volumes to reach the piano keys. I still remember that solo too. I was 3. If I had to learn that solo in 33 steps, I would not have been able to do that.

Six steps. Really.

Now just because there are only six steps doesn't mean it is an easy process. Simple and easy do not usually go together. Let's take a closer look at these simple steps:

Discovery

Discovery is what sparks curiosity. You know the 3-year-old that is asking "Why?" all the time is trying to connect cause to effect. Isn't that fascinating?! How often do we ask that question? We often discourage that question with the reply, "That's not important. All you have to do is remember what I'm telling you." What if it <u>is</u> important?

Let's take this a step further. What if discovering the answer for himself is just as important as the answer?

"Why does bread rise?" asks little Ben as he punches down the dough.

"Hmmm, I don't know. Let's find out."

You get out a really old cookbook that used caked yeast instead of dry. It says to mix a bit of flour, sugar, and warm water then add the yeast.

"Oooo! Bubbles!"

Then you try flour, salt, and warm water. Nothing happens. After the yeast in the sugar mixture is done bubbling, you pour the goop out. Then taste the stuff that is coating the bowl. It's not sweet anymore.

"Do we see bubbles in the dough?"

Ben answers, "YES!" (3-year-olds always yell answers...) "What does that mean?"

"YEAST MAKES BUBBLES OUT OF SUGAR!"

"But bubbles are hard to cut and eat, and peanut butter gets all gooey. What holds the bubbles together?"

"FLOUR!!!"

This process sparks the child's curiosity and because he has figured out the answer for himself, he will retain it longer.

This process has unintended consequences too. If the child knows that every time that he asks a question about anything, he gets to do an experiment, he will be less inclined to ask and more likely to discover things for himself.

One of the most annoying bosses I had would answer all my questions with, "Where did you look first? And then? And then? Oh, you didn't look there? Look there." I wanted an answer that wouldn't take any time or effort on my part. The result? I would have needed him to give me the answer every time I faced that situation. If he <u>had</u> given me the answer right away, I wouldn't have internalized it. It's funny; in all my communications with him over the years, he always adds, "Let me know how I can help you!" to all his notes. I think to myself, what he *really* means is, "Let me know how I can help you *and I'll ask you questions so you remember where to look.*"

The important thing about Discovery is spending the time it takes to get into all the details you need to satisfy your curiosity. Does this new stuff catch your imagination? Does it chase you in your sleep? How long do you wait to start looking into it? Most adults don't ask "Why?" or "How?" or "What?" immediately as children do. They have to wait for the opportune moment. They must check with their peers or their supervisor to get permission to be curious.

In the Workbook exercise that follows we will go through the steps together so you can see how it works.

First, we need to choose a project. Here are some examples:

- Learn five phrases in a foreign language.
- Learn five steps in a dance
- Learn how to cook/bake something new
- Start a blog
- Sew something, cross stitch something, or crochet something
- Write a description of your favorite place

The possibilities are endless, but the project has to spark your interest. A question to ask yourself is this: What have I always wanted to do but never took the time?

My grandson loves dinosaurs, and he knows at least 20 species. He was 8 when he started. Here I am, an old granny, and I knew about five. He challenged me to learn some more, so I got into the book he recommended, and I picked up another fifteen species. Then I got curious and got online. I focused on just Cretaceous, then on just herbivores. I looked up and it was after 2:00 AM! I now know way too much about Cretaceous Era herbivores. Since this is not currently something I use, I do not doubt that the information will fade. But for about twenty minutes, my grandson thought I was a genius.

Once you try something on your own, you have a better understanding of what your child goes through. Experiment with your first project.

Workbook Exercise

<u>**My First Project:**</u>

_____

_____

_____

Now that you have a project, we move on to the first step.

<u>Step 1: Discovery/What do I already know?</u>

After you have discovered what you want to learn, you need to find out what you already know. Here's the hard part. How do you get your child to be curious about the right things? Well, first of all, that's not your job. Children are naturally curious. First graders may jump from dinosaurs to planets to Taekwondo to horticulture. That is fine. Can you use any of those subjects to teach reading, math, and writing? Of course! You don't have to tell them "Well, now it's time for your math class, so put down your book." Say, for instance, that they're studying dinosaurs. Ask them when they lived. Then ask them how long that period was, then ask them any questions with numbers in them. Draw a graph. Compare sizes. How heavy was a tyrannosaur? What, currently, is the heaviest land animal? How do they compare?

Have the child write a report and give it at dinner time! Don't forget to clap!

What do you already know? We want to see what we have that can apply to what we're discovering. What skills, vocabulary, processes, or knowledge do we already possess?

1. How is this related to anything you've studied?

   _____

   _____

2. How is this related to any activity or experience you've had?

   _____

   _____

3. What do you recognize?

   _____

   _____

You may have thought that you cannot mix reading and history, or history and math, or science and geometry...Completely Wrong! Everything is connected! Beware though, once you start your child on this curiosity path, you've let the tiger out of the cage!

Step 2: Explore/Try to use this material

Now, we jump into it. We read it, we listen to it, we try it. If you're learning a new language, you can buy a romance novel or young adult novel in that language and try to read it. These books are written for a 10-12-year-old audience, so they won't be very complex grammatically or with vocabulary. You may have to be looking up every other word at first, but you will soon be looking up fewer words. You will gain some sense of the vocabulary and grammar from the context. If, however, the book doesn't use the same alphabet, you will also discover that shortly as well. You have a starting point!

You begin by learning the representational part of the language, the art of its writing. Here's an example:

It's a beautiful day!

É um lindo dia! (Portuguese)

C'est une belle journée! (French)

Es ist ein schöner Tag! (German)

All use a recognizable alphabet with a few variations.

Прекрасный день! (Russian)

Είναι μια όμορφη μέρα! (Greek)

這是美好的一天！(Chinese)

إنه يوم جميل! (Arabic)

Each of those languages uses different alphabets (obviously) and the direction of the writing may be left to right or right to left! What would be your next step? Consider how you learned to read your native language? Elementary school grammar books, right? Wouldn't it make sense then that you could use the ones they use to teach their youngest children how to read? They usually come with pictures and ways to remember what sounds go with which symbols. What have you done just now? You have used the information you *already have* to discover a way to assimilate a new language.

In the "Try It" step, we try using the new information. We want to test our understanding of it to see if there are gaps. Well, if it's new, there had better be gaps! What we do in this step is locate the gaps to find out what we DON'T know. This is the "Isn't That interesting!" point where we determine what to tackle first. We need to make note of these things that are missing in our experience, our knowledge, or our skills.

You've tried it now. What have you discovered? Write down in a couple of sentences what you have problems with.

The following things need to be improved:

1. _____

_____

2. _____

_____

3. _____

_____

Step 3: Analysis

We must now take an analytical approach to these gaps.

1. Are these subjects related to things we know but have used under different circumstances?
2. Are they physical skills that require specialized training?
3. Are they mental skills that prompt us to input more information?
4. Are they mental skills that require a different perspective and manipulation of available information?

5. Are they emotional components that may change our perspective?

6. Is there a leap of faith that might connect things that aren't normally associated?

You can see that a lot goes into this phase of the learning process. There is a saying, "Math was a whole lot more fun until the alphabet got involved!" You can recognize that the gap, in that case, is a perspective challenge.

Unless a person gets to the crux of the problem, (the problem behind the problem that's under the problem that you didn't recognize before) it's harder to bridge that gap.

I think the hardest part of the Analysis is asking the right questions. When we get past the place where our experiences can help us, we might need to get a coach or a teacher to get a second look. All you need from them is their expertise in observation. The best help is always what you have within you though. If it comes from you, it stays with you. If it comes from an outside source, you have to keep going to someone else for the answers.

If you get stuck at this juncture, you're not alone. When was the first time you were without a definitive answer to a situation? For most of us, it was when we were trying to choose between the red bike and the blue bike. As we progress through school and life, it always comes down to two choices: my way or the highway. The customer is always right. The boss is always right. The teacher is always right. We haven't had to rely on our own resourcefulness. Where do people go for that ultimate decision-maker, the ultimate source of information, the purveyor of truth? Tell me it's not Facebook.

Take a look at what you wrote down for things to work on. Now ask yourself, "How can I break down these difficulties into manageable steps? What books can I read? What videos can I watch? Who has done what I'm attempting? Can I ask them for an opinion or an observation of what I'm doing? What things have I done before are related to what I'm trying now?

Here is a start:

1. What is the nature of the difficulty?

   _____

   _____

2. What are my resources?

   _____

   _____

3. How can I break this problem down into smaller pieces?

   _____

   _____

4. What is my perspective on the problem?

   _____

   _____

Now, you can get much more detailed than this. Later, you can come up with more questions as you get deeper into your project. Remember that show, "The X Files?" What was their slogan? "The truth is out there." *What if it isn't out there?* What if the truth is within you? What if that's where the ultimate source of information is? Who has to make the final decision? You do. If you take on that responsibility, don't you then have more control? More autonomy? More freedom? More than two choices?

If you need to find this inner truth, this inner resourcefulness, the only outward thing you need is someone that knows what questions to ask to get you to your inner truth. That's what the Fegan Method provides.

Working with me gives you access to someone that knows the questions you need to consider that allows you to find answers. You can contact me at https://www.feganmethod.com/

Step 4: Focus

At this point, we're filling in gaps. When we did our analysis in Step 3, we looked at the "Why" part of the equation. Now we look at the "How" part.

Whatever you're striving to learn, there's a book, a video, a CD, or a seminar that can give you information. Make sure the information is factual and helpful! We have already discussed what we currently are aware of: the skills we already have and some of the appropriate information from Step 2. We have to decide if we need more facts/data/information, physical ability, or philosophical acuity. (I get my $20-words for the week in that sentence!) You know the information dump because that's what you got in school. You may have gotten the physical ability education in school, in special classes, or with a coach. But what the heck is Philosophical acuity? Philosophy is a love (philo) of learning or wisdom (sophy). There were two schools of thought in ancient Greece.

The Sophists of old were very fond of wisdom, but the most popular expression of this ideology was quoting *other* people's ideas. The Stoics of old were also very fond of wisdom, but their pursuit of knowledge was empirical—facts, information, and logic.

What difference does that make in learning? Well, the purpose of those educational philosophies was to make better citizens— wise, informed, well-rounded people with impeccable ethics. Basic education included the disciplines of communication and mathematics on the academic side, and music and physical prowess on the physical side. Philosophy was "higher" education, and Philosophical Accuity was how well you saw past the surface concerns.

How does becoming a better communicator help a mathematician? How can they possibly be related? Let me put it to you this way: Who do you think would be the best at understanding poetry—a language expert or a math expert? Language, right? Maybe? What is common though? Poets deal with abstract concepts through figurative language. $A=Bx + C$ is pretty figurative! Who do you think would be better at figuring out mathematical word problems? It might be the language expert! Who in the math world likes word problems? Nobody? Why? Because those problems deal with the real world. The language experts understand because they can follow the plot and the setting and determine the necessary information to arrive at an answer, right? Who are the players? Who needs to count their oranges? Why do we need to know when those two trains meet? Language people do that regularly!

What this Fegan Method seeks to attain is connections between disciplines. For instance: the gap between your current skills as a basketball player and those of a varsity starter might be solved by investigating ballet. The gap between your current ability to communicate and getting on a TEDx Talk may be grasping a technical aspect of giving a presentation. You may have to move beyond wordcraft and body language into the use of pictures and demonstrations with the use of videos, photos, and animated graphs. What I mean is that *any* experience you've had throughout your life, *any* expertise you have acquired, and *any* insight you've developed can be useful in closing those gaps.

Once you have a handle on your untapped wealth of resourcefulness, you engage in targeted practice to enhance your new skills and knowledge to the point where it becomes second nature.

This targeted practice is not what you think it is. When you're learning an instrument and the teacher says, "Go home and practice!" do you go home and play through the song one hundred times? Most do. What are the results? They will get the first part and the last part of the song learned and foul up the middle every time.

The same thing will happen when cramming for a test. I was in the library at college when I heard a girl crying. She was in my history class (American History 1865 to the Present), so I went over to see what was wrong. She was studying for her history final (as was I) and she had gone through her book and highlighted every single word of the chapters we were testing on. She was, in effect, trying to memorize the book. And she was doing it by reading the same 85 pages over and over again. In contrast, I used the targeted practice approach. I focused my studies on the aspects of the less familiar material and, as a result, read the equivalent of five pages instead of 85. I reviewed my notes and applied what I had learned in discussions and essays regarding the information on the topic at hand. I was done in about two hours, and she pulled an all-nighter. She went into the final having slept only three hours over the previous two days. She did not pass. I did. I wish I could say I studied with her, and we both passed the next test, but she dropped out of school.

Targeted practice means you work on the new material only. You play with it, turn it around, upside down, inside out. You change the colors; you do it backward. You become familiar with the new material. You do not go back to the beginning and run through it one hundred times. How would practicing something you already do well help you to learn the stuff you are unfamiliar with?

How do you go about targeted practice?

1. What have I tried?

   _____

   _____

2. How else can I examine this gap?

   _____

   _____

3. Have I done something similar? How did I solve that problem?

    _____

    _____

4. If the gap is wide, how do I reduce it to manageable pieces?

    _____

    _____

As an example, if you're learning to fly a plane, you go up with an instructor (because if you go up without an instructor you may not get to the second step of the process!) and you learn how all the instruments work. Then you learn how to turn, ascend, and descend. You won't solo on your first lesson! You may spend time in a flight simulator to learn the nuances of take-offs and landings. But you are only working on the take-offs and landings at first. So, you won't solo on your second lesson either. See? We add one skill at a time, so you get a cognitive understanding of the process and then a physical sensation to tell you when it is right. Every time you fly, you get more experience: how it looks, sounds, and feels. It forms the basis for all your instincts. Unless you internalize all these inputs, you cannot solo. Your instructor will not take the test for you. All the information has to come from within YOU. Gradually, the gaps get fewer and smaller.

Step 5: Integration

In this step, we start the integration process…stringing all the old and new information together.

Think of it as if you were walking out on an icy pond. You are not sure how deep the ice goes. It might crack and break, so you go from what you are sure is thick enough to hold your weight, test the next part then move from there.

You are moving from a place of comfort to a place that though you may have mastered it, seems relatively new and uncertain. In most cases, you must slow down to test how smooth the transition from old material to new material is. You must give yourself the time to see enough ahead to prepare for the newer material. It's like the difference between looking at the hood ornament and looking at the road ahead when you're driving.

1. What is the last place where I feel comfortable before I use the new material?

   _____

   _____

2. How do I transition from what I know to what is new smoothly?

_____

_____

3. How do I gradually speed up the process so I cannot tell where the break between the old and new stuff is?

_____

_____

4. How does it feel when I get it right?

_____

_____

You repeat this process at every incidence of new material and in doing so, you might determine that the gap has not been adequately filled. At that point, you repeat the 2nd, 3rd, and 4th steps to fill the gap then you go back to step 5 to integrate the new stuff again, carefully.

How do we illustrate this step? Let's play a game of soccer!

You are not a beginner; you've seen soccer games on television or maybe live.

(Step 1) You know that there are different positions for all the players, and you know how points are scored. You have a basic understanding of kicking the ball down the pitch and scoring. So you try it.

(Step 2) Now you find out it's difficult to run down the pitch and dribble when other people are trying to take the ball away from you. You aren't accurate on passes. You don't know how to handle the ball when it's passed to you. Now you know what you don't know.

(Step 3) You determine that you have to start with being able to dribble with both feet. This will allow you to move the ball down the pitch and pass with either foot and reduce the chances of a member of the other team stealing the ball. You start by dribbling down the pitch alternating feet. One foot is definitely more controlled and more accurate than the other. You close your eyes and examine what it feels like to dribble correctly. What is the foot position relative to the ball? How does your running speed affect the accuracy of the kicks? What are your eyes looking at when you dribble correctly? Can you look down the pitch while you're dribbling? Once you know what you see and what you feel when you're dribbling properly with your strong foot, you try to reproduce that in the weaker foot. You dribble down the pitch with just your weaker foot, working one skill at a time.

(Step 4) You start by running slowly and kicking the ball with the correct part of the foot. You do this several times, increasing your running speed each time. This may take several days. Next, you concentrate on your visual training. You start slowly again so that you can concentrate on the new material... where to look. You are striving to improve your peripheral vision, so you don't have to move your head to see your kick and simultaneously see your target. How would you use this skill in a game? How would it improve your ability to pass? How would it affect your reactions to the other team's defense? In what way could you see this visual skill improving your shooting ability?

(Step 5) Now that you can dribble with your weaker foot, and keep your head up, you work on alternating kicks down the pitch. You are integrating what you have learned into your larger pattern of behavior. The more you run up and down the pitch dribbling, the better you get, the more instinctive you get, and the more complex moves you can make. And each time you add a new move to your repertoire, you do it the same way...slowly doing steps 2 through 5 until you are a beast at moving the ball.

Obviously, you might need help with some of the steps. A good initial action is recording your performance. It teaches you how to become self-aware. You might want to watch really good players and see what they do. You could enlist the help of a good soccer coach to develop some practice scenarios that would solidify the new information. Everyone's learning style will be different so you may have to go through several coaches to find one that speaks your learning language. But regardless of the coach and the way he works with you, you continue to think of these steps as you improve.

Step 6: Resolution

This is the step that is nearly always left undone. And yet it is the most important step! When I have my music students go through these steps, at the 2nd step, they must **circle** the mistake they're making. When they have completed steps 3, 4, and 5, they must ***erase that circle as part of the resolution.***

People will react two different ways when confronted with their "circles".

1. They will come to the circled area and think to themselves "This is where I always mess up. It's that HARD part." This sends the command to the brain that

indicates a rule has been made. "This is the place where you are supposed to mess up." The brain, eager to please, then dutifully sends incorrect information to the body which causes a wrong note. The brain says, "Success! We messed it up for you just as the rule says!" Then the person listens to the resulting cacophony and despairs because he's practiced it so much and it's still wrong!

2. They will come to the circled area and ignore it. They will also ignore any other circled areas, regardless of whether they have been resolved. It may or may not be resolved!

The idea is to erase the circle and say, "This has been learned and now it is the most beautiful part of the song." Why? Very often the most beautiful part of a musical selection will be the most difficult because it is also the part that elicits the greatest emotion. Isn't this true of almost everything in life?

It's that sweet spot in the racket as you put the topspin onto the tennis ball to the right rear corner of the court at faster-than-sound velocity while the opponent stares helplessly!

It's using a <u>pen</u> to finish the mathematics test and getting a 100% score!

It's taking a 4-hour certification test in 2 ½ hours and passing it the first time when the average person must take it three or four times and use the entire four hours to get a passing grade.

It's finding that perfect word to finish the last line of the poem so that when people read it, they are brought to tears.

It is giving that persuasive speech that gets the audience on its feet and racing to buy your book at the back of the room.

There is no feeling like it.

What effect do you think this feeling of accomplishment would have on your child? How would it feel to know that whatever school they go to, whatever line of work they choose, your children will never be left behind? What confidence would they gain and what level do you think their self-esteem would be?

The last step: I can now do

_____

_____

_____

_____

…as if I have done it all my life. I really enjoy being able to do this because

_____

_____

_____

I am going to give you one last example: My son, Sean.

Sean's story:

My son was distraught. He had to take Summer School again. He pretended it was nothing, but I could tell he was frustrated.

We were informed by a letter from the school stating that Sean had flunked English, Math, and Biology and would have to register for Summer School to make up the classes so he could be promoted to Eighth Grade. My first question to him was, "How in the heck do you fail your native language?"

I contacted the school so he could get registered for the classes. He needed to go for four weeks in June, two hours per subject, and they didn't offer Biology. That would mean four hours per day, four days a week. That's thirty-two hours of study for each subject. I wondered how thirty-two hours of concentrated study could replace one hundred fifty hours of class time. Summer School doesn't use the regular grading system; it makes use of the Pass/Fail assessment. At the end of the session, he passed, but he wasn't reading or doing math at the seventh-grade level.

We did an assessment test, and he was on the *fourth-grade* level for most of his math skills, and yet he was officially promoted to eighth grade. I asked him if he wanted to get caught up. He was pretty sure it was impossible, but he wanted to try.

So, in July and the first part of August, we studied math using this method. In six weeks, he had brought up his skills to seventh-grade level.

At that point, we decided to home-school for eighth grade. His teachers were aghast! "He needs to socialize with people his own age! He can't go from structured classes to unstructured chaos and learn what he needs to! You will make this situation even worse! You must be in denial because his test scores indicate that he's incapable of advanced thought!"

Did I mention that on the Iowa Basic Skills (IBS) tests, he was in the twentieth percentile? That would indicate that Sean had the mind of a fourth-grader. The teachers all assumed it would never improve. I found it funny they would consider this since he never had Individualized Education Programs throughout his elementary and junior high education.

I nodded to the naysayers and mumbled under my breath, "We'll see." Luckily Sean was unaware of how low his teachers thought his prospects were.

We started with a theme for the school year: Lewis and Clark's bicentenary celebration of their historic trip up the Missouri River. Many of the sites they visited were within a few miles of where we lived. We used the integrated approach and the six steps throughout our studies. We even went to Nebraska City to go to the Lewis and Clark Museum and got to board a replica of the boat they used!

At the end of our school year, Sean informed me that he wanted to join the high school band in ninth grade. To be readmitted to the public school system, he had to take an assessment test to prove he had the requisite knowledge and skills needed to operate at the ninth-grade level. "How ironic," he said, "that I have to test to get into ninth grade, but had I been in public school eighth grade, whether I was competent or not, all I had to do was pass and take Summer School again."

I discovered that the reason he tested so low on his IBS tests was not that he wasn't intelligent enough, he just didn't know how to take tests. Well, with all the studying and tests he took, and because of the six-step method, he was now well-prepared.

Four weeks later, the results came in. Most of the general areas showed remarkable improvements. He jumped from fourth-grade level in general math skills to tenth grade. He jumped from sixth-grade level in English grammar and reading comprehension to twelfth grade. In some of the individual skills, he was rated PHS. PHS? What the heck was that? Down at the bottom of the report in teeny tiny font, it said, PHS was Post High School. Some footnotes indicated he'd improved his ability by **ten grades**. You read that correctly. Instead of being mentally stunted at the fourth-grade level, he was several years beyond his peers.

After much discussion, we decided **not** to go back to the junior high teachers that said home-schooling was a danger to his academic and social health and wave the results under their noses. But it certainly was tempting.

Conclusion:

How do you think he felt? He had been treated as a chronically low achiever and discounted throughout most of his school life. There was that feeling of helplessness and the belief (false belief it seems!) that he would never be able to solve his internal learning problems or direct his life. There was the additional false belief that he could never amount to anything.

Before we started homeschooling that fall, he confessed that he didn't understand why it didn't take eight hours of school to finish all the subjects he was taking: Math, English grammar and literature, History, Sciences, Taekwondo, and Saxophone. He was getting nearly all of his studies done before noon, and the Taekwondo course was taught in the evening. He doubted he would be sufficiently caught up by the time the year ended. He did not discover that he had to take an assessment test to get into ninth grade until May, at the end of his eighth-grade year. He was convinced that he would have to take Summer School for the rest of his years in high school.

You should have seen his face when we got the results back! This undeserved treatment, however, has had a lasting effect. His default thinking goes to "I'm not good enough or smart enough to do this. Why do I try?" when things don't go his way. Now, at age thirty-one, he doesn't do that as much. He is much more confident and self-assured. He spent four years in the army and even went to Afghanistan for a tour of duty. He now realizes that the labels placed on him in his formative years by the educational system he trusted to give him the knowledge and skills he needed to be a productive citizen did exactly the opposite.

I often wonder how many other students find themselves in this situation. I hope I've given you a glimmer of optimism after reading this book.

This method works with any age. I've taught students from age three to seventy-eight in nearly any area of study you could name: from kindergarten to college, from ballet to football, from arithmetic to college-level calculus. I know it has worked for me when I had to master new areas of study. I have a degree in Music Education, and one in Business Finance. I am certified in Life Insurance and Debt Analysis. I am an Investment Adviser Representative which is the top tier of stockbrokers. I am a certified John Maxwell Speaker/Trainer/Coach. I have been a truck stop cook, a ballet teacher, an author, and a Toastmaster. I am an accredited coach and founding member of the Conscious Coaching Academy and recognized by the European Mentoring and Coaching Council.

I know this method works. There is too much evidence to deny. DO NOT wait for things to get better. It's too important! Contact me through the website below.

For a fuller discussion on how to implement these simple steps, you can book a one-on-one interview, then join one of our online learning courses, or schedule group or one-on-one coaching to work with you on an ongoing basis.

Contact me at: https://www.feganmethod.com/

Frequently Asked Questions

1. **How can you be sure it works with everything?**

    Every time a person learns something, anything, the information gets put into storage. Part of the beauty of this method is that it draws from information you already have to learn something new. There is no such thing as a blank slate.

2. **What if you get stuck?**

    It is unusual for anyone to learn something new without getting stuck at least once. It doesn't mean you've failed; it just means you may have to take a different approach. There are all sorts of resources available from books and videos to private coaching sessions to help you get unstuck!

3. **How can I teach this to my 5-year-old?**

    We vastly underestimate the mental and physical power of children. This is funny because we know some toddlers that could rule the world! It won't take long for your child to catch the drift of how to learn anything and apply this process to everything! Just ask THEM questions and allow them to explore the possibilities. If it works with 3-year-olds, it will work with your kindergartner.

4. Does this only work for children?

Of course not! I've been using this system for over 65 years. My father was using this system until he was 85 years old.

I'm not asking you to trust me on this; I'm asking you to test me. I know it works!

Contact me at https://www.feganmethod.com/

Feel free to copy and use the following workbook any time you want--either with your kids or for yourself! We know children learn more by watching and if your children see you using this as a guide to learn something new, and you're excited about it and share it with them, they'll be more inclined to love learning too.

Workbook

Project:_____

_____

_____

What do you already know?

1. How is this related to anything you've studied?

   _____

   _____

2. How is this related to any activity or experience you've had?

   _____

   _____

3. What do you recognize?

   _____

   _____

The following things need to be improved:

1. _____

   _____

2. _____

   _____

3. _____

_____

Analyze what we don't know:

1. What is the nature of the difficulty?

_____

_____

2. What are my resources?

_____

_____

3. How can I break this problem down into smaller pieces?

_____

_____

4. What is my perspective on the problem?

_____

_____

Targeted practice

1. What have I tried?

_____

_____

2. How else can I examine this gap?

_____

_____

3. Have I done something similar? How did I solve that problem?

_____

_____

4. If the gap is wide, how do I reduce it to manageable pieces?

_____

_____

Transitions:

1. What is the last place where I feel comfortable before I use the new material?

_____

_____

2. How do I transition from what I know to what is new smoothly?

_____

_____

3. How do I gradually speed up the process so I cannot tell where the break between the old and new stuff is?

_____

_____

4. How does it feel when I get it right?

_____

_____

—

Certificate

YOU DID IT!!!

DATE

SIGNATURE

Printed in the USA
CPSIA information can be obtained
at www.ICGtesting.com
LVHW040111070624
782493LV00002B/548

9 781387 430116